Stella

Stella

Stella Warigi

MythicQull Publishing

Chapter 1: Introduction

My name is Stella Wanjiru Warigi. I was born on December 22, 2002 in Kenya. My mother is Beatrice Warigi Njoroge. I have a dad but I don't know him. I was raised by a single mom. I have two younger siblings who are Shantel and James.

When I was born, my mother did not have enough money so she decided to go and work as a nanny in urban areas in Kenya. I had to live with my grandmother. She took care of me and raised me as her daughter until I became old enough to join school.

I attended Gachiku Primary School from kindergarten up to eighth grade. While there, I participated in sports such as racing and pole vault. I was on an honor roll student and received an academic achievement award. The school enabled me to grow academically and as a person, teaching me high moral standards.

Chapter 2: High School Education

Later, I attended Immaculate Girls High School. I was able to leave my grandma and go to Nairobi to stay with my mom and attend High School.

In High School I participated in racing. Racing is a competition of speed in which competitors try to complete a given task in the shortest amount of time. It makes me comfortable and is enjoyable. I won the races up to a good level.

While in high school my step-father had high expectations that put a lot of pressure on me to succeed in school. He did this because he was paying my school fees and didn't want his money to be wasted.

Chapter 3: College

When it was time for college, I chose to go to Jewel Professional College. I chose the college because it is a Christian based school and highly academic.

I talked to my step-dad about joining the college. I hoped he would support me in paying the fees, but he ignored me.

Instead I let my mom know that I was going to study and pursue my career. I promised her that I would study and make her proud. I didn't have worries of not succeeding. She sent me to college with high expectations that I would make her proud.

I joined college and chose a course in hospitality management. I chose this major course because it was my hobby.

Throughout college life, I didn't join any outside activities. I managed to finish my courses and passed well. I graduated with a degree in Hospitality Management.

While in college I also managed to study foreign languages such as German and Korean. I hoped that one day I might travel to those countries.

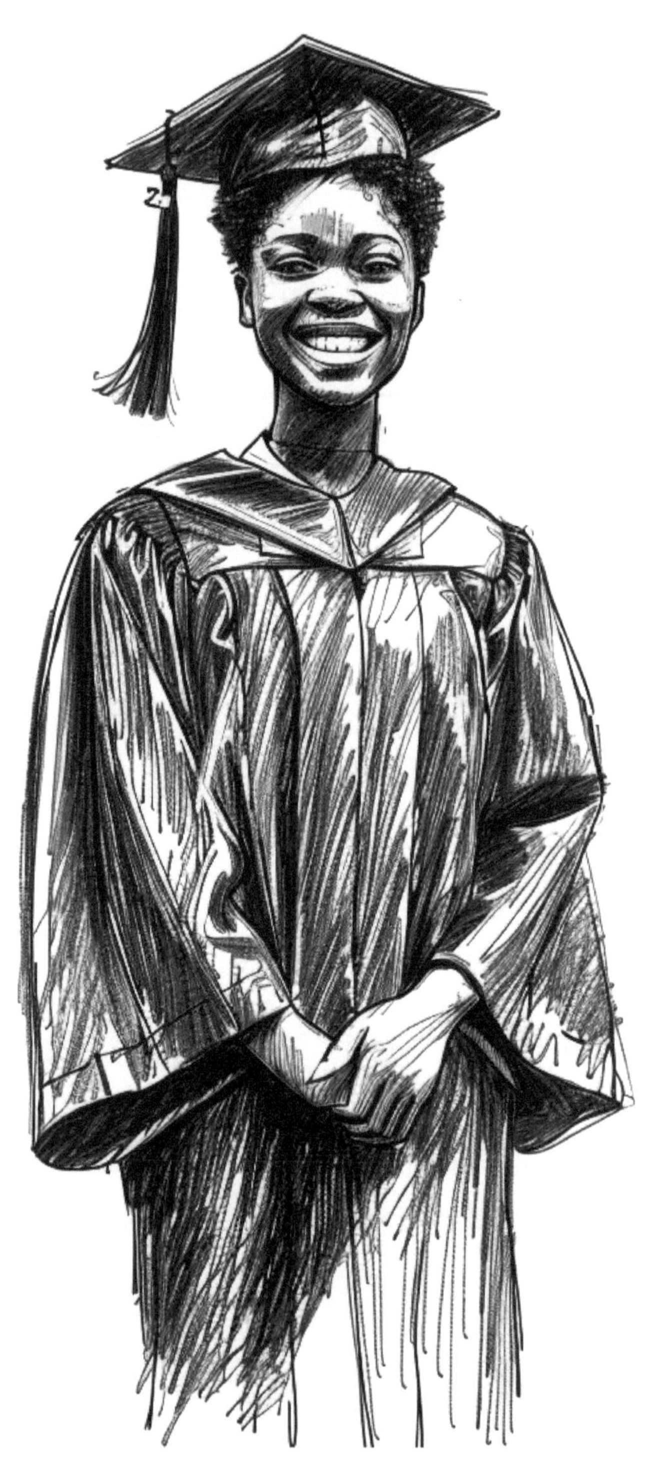

Chapter 4: After College

After college I started a small business that would give me my own upkeep. I sold adult clothes. The business had downs and ups; sometimes I sold a lot and other times I wouldn't even sell a single cloth.

I managed to provide for myself, though it was a tough time.

In that life of hustling, I met a man named Hamphury and fell in love with him. He was very caring and protective. He really took care of me until he got me pregnant.

We started having issues because he claimed he didn't love me anymore. I wasn't ready for marriage yet because I didn't have a stable job that would cater for me and the baby. I decided that the baby and I wouldn't stay with Hamphury.

I wasn't able to work while pregnant, so I continued staying with my parents. They felt very disappointed with me, but they couldn't change the situation that I was pregnant.

Chapter 5: Birth

It was a tough time for me carrying the pregnancy. The labor pain came early and I delivered when I was seven months along.

The delivery time was really good, though. I didn't strain a lot. The doctors took good care of me.

I didn't manage to get an ultrasound during the pregnancy, so I was surprised when I gave birth to twin girls.

I told Hamphury that God had blessed us with two twin girls, but he rejected me. He left me in the hospital full of pain. He said I lied to him because I delivered preterm kids and also that they don't have twins in their family, so the babies couldn't be his. I had to bear the consequences alone.

I was so happy to have my twins. They are blessings from God. I named them Nilsa Njeri and Melissa Wanjiku. They are so sweet! I said to myself, "I won't get rid of them but I will take care of them fully."

Chapter 6: Parenting

After the twins were born, I didn't have many challenges because my parents were very supportive as usual. My mom had to leave her business and stay home to take care of me and the babies. May God bless her abundantly!

When the kids were old enough, I had to take care of them myself.

I started searching for job opportunities but it was very tough to find one. I just tried to hustle and get something small, but found nothing because I was too young.

Life became really tough for me. I sacrificed a lot for my kids to have a good life.

When my daughters were one year and two months old, I found another man. On appearances he looked like a good man to me. He promised he would take care of me and the kids. Because I was desperate, I agreed.

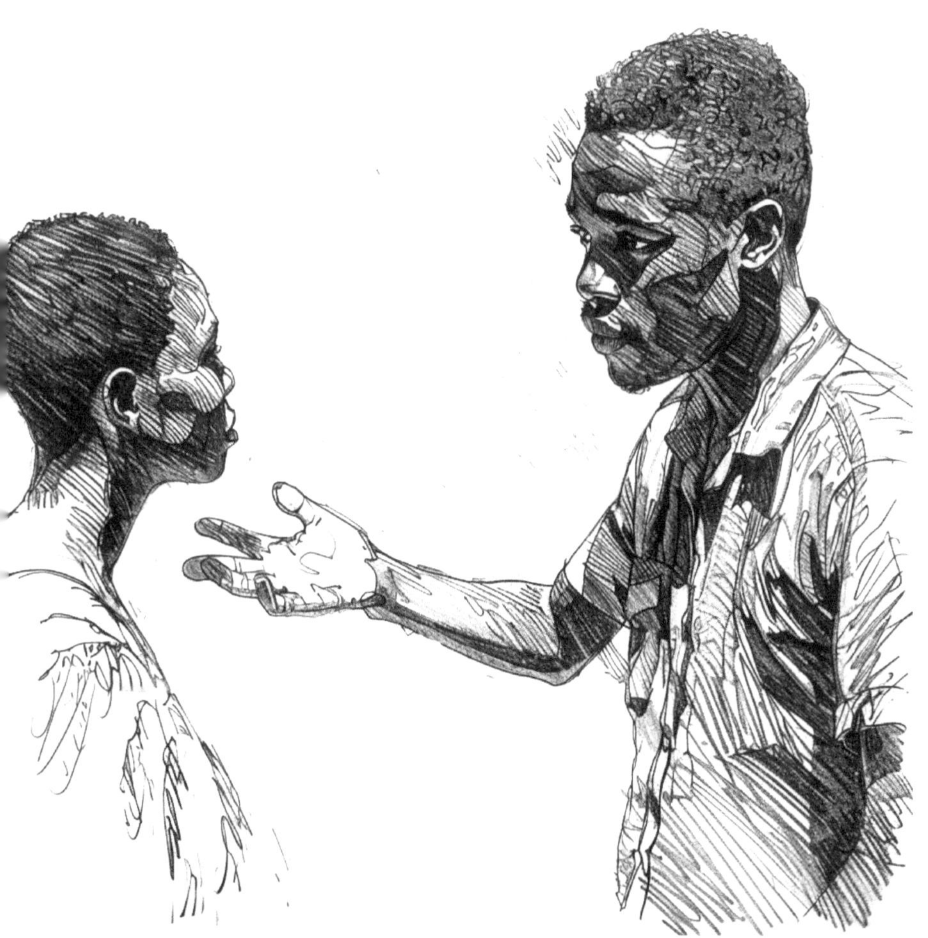

He got me pregnant again. WAAAH!
It was a tough moment for me
because I wasn't ready to raise
another child. The man disappeared
and left me alone not knowing what
to do and where to start.

I was in painful tears. Depression attacked me. I took a step toward terminating the pregnancy before my mom found out.

I tried so hard to make money for the abortion medication. Remember I was jobless so I had to struggle to find the money. If I didn't get any money, what would I do?

I continued keeping the pregnancy secret from my parents and the society, too.

Chapter 7: Illness

Unfortunately, Satan attacked my kids with an illness I never imagined called convulsions. I rushed them to the nearby Health Centre. Their condition got worse, so they had to be taken to the National Hospital for admission and proper medication.

They were admitted to Kenyatta
National Hospital in Nairobi. They
were treated and taken care of.
Nilsa got more sick. She was taken
to an emergency room for further
check up and to use oxygen.

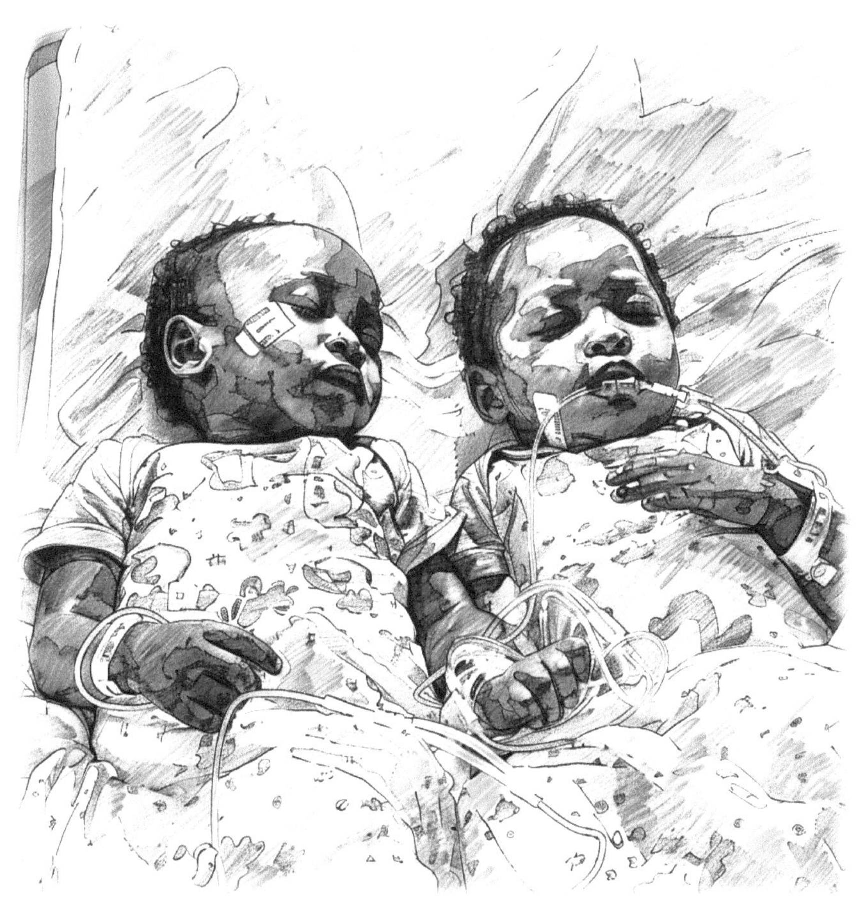

I was really stressed. There was nothing I could do but to tell God to remember my daughters.

The girls were moved to separate rooms. I wouldn't be able to look after them both myself. I had to call my cousin to help with one of the girls.

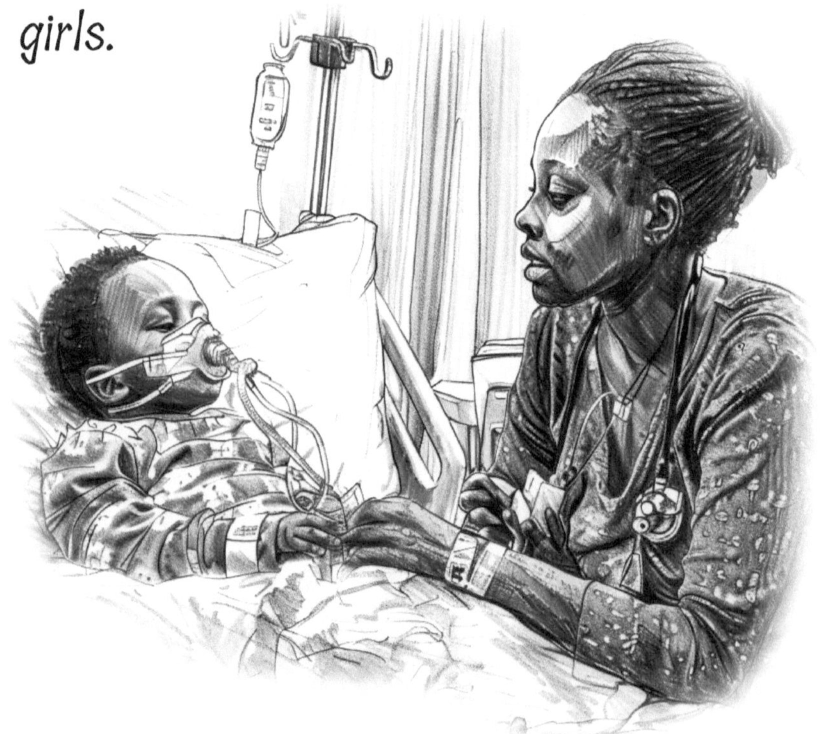

Chapter 8: Healing

Nilsa was weak. She was not talking nor standing, or even sitting down on her own. It was another tough moment for me, but God gave me strength to take care of her.

We started doing physical therapy on her. She did very well. I glorify God for that.

Nilsa recovered slow by slow. Both girls were discharged from the hospital. They recovered fully through the power of healing from the Almighty.

The next step was to find out how much the hospital bill would cost. The bill was 146,000ksh!

I didn't have that kind of money and insurance had not matured yet, so it couldn't help.

I had to talk to a social worker to help me. I met them there in the hospital. They usually help those people who are not able to pay the bill. God was there with me.

The social worker listened and managed to assist where they could. They paid half of the bill and the other half, I have to pay in little amounts until it's over.

Chapter 9: Change

I decided to keep my baby instead of terminating the pregnancy because I remembered I had learned in my Christian school that's a crime. Before God, I would be a killer.

For a time, I wanted to give the baby up for adoption. I felt like I had no other option at all. I didn't want the baby to come and suffer in my hands because I had no money to raise it together with my other kids.

While trying to find someone to adopt the baby on social media, I came across a lady called Heather from United States. I told her my story. She listened and gave me words of hope. I really treasure that woman a lot. She was God sent.

After talking to Heather, I decided not to give the baby up for adoption. Instead, I will raise it no matter what happens.

And that is how my life began again.

Chapter 10: Gratitude

On May 15th 2024 at 11:30 am, the labor started. I was rushed to the hospital immediately. At 1:00 pm my bouncing baby girl arrived.

I was very happy. I didn't imagine the baby would bring so much happiness to my life again. I accepted the baby and her name will be Vanessa Muthoni.

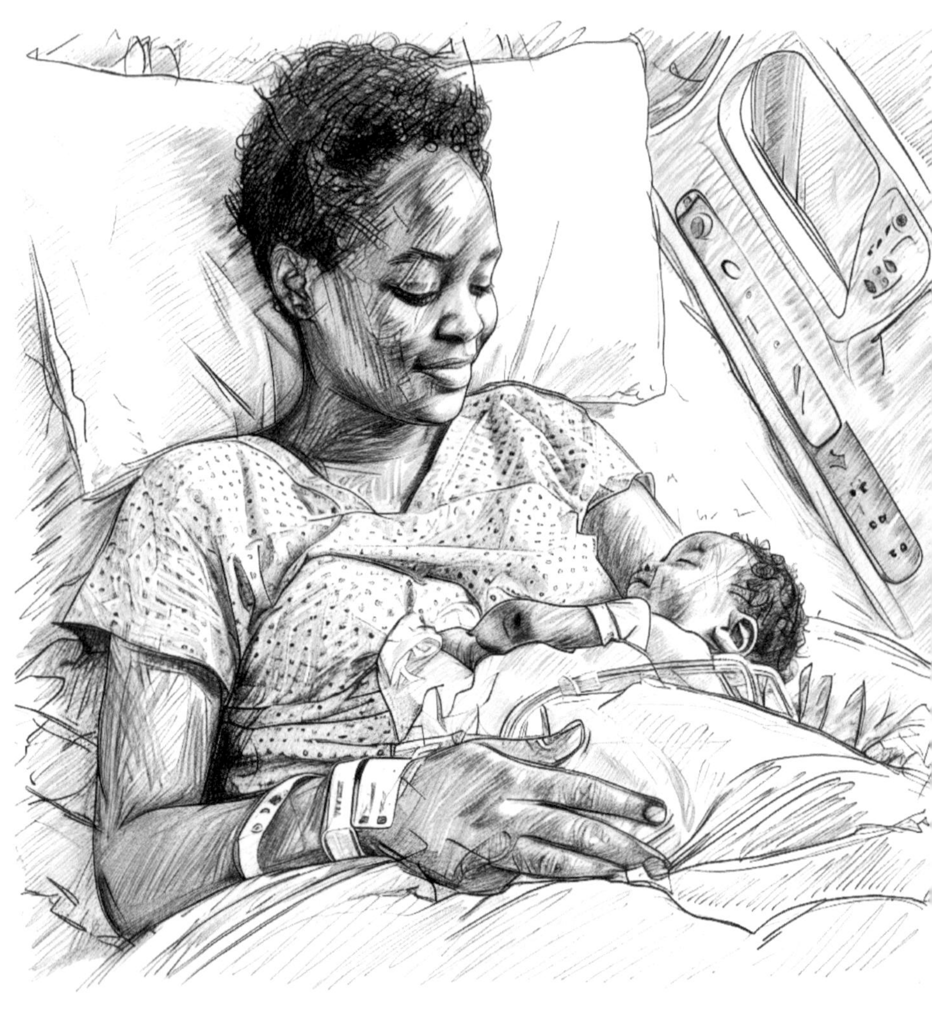

I am done with having kids. God has blessed me with enough. Now, my focus is on making money to raise all my kids.

That's my story for now. I am a 23 year old girl, suffering a lot, but I am a strong woman, too. I am trying to do small business to keep myself busy and provide my upkeep. I cook fried potatoes. In Kenya, we call them chips. My business is running smoothly.

My message for you is that, in every tough situation that you go through, never forget to tell God thank you each and every time.